Chapter 1: Mastering Risk Management for Trading Success

Understanding Risk: The Foundation of Trading

In this section, we will delve into the fundamental concept of risk and its significance in trading. By thoroughly understanding and effectively managing risk, you can enhance your chances of achieving trading success. This section will provide you with a solid foundation in risk management, ensuring you approach the market with a cautious and informed mindset.

1.1 The Concept of Risk

Risk is an inherent aspect of trading. It refers to the potential for losses or adverse outcomes that may occur when participating in financial markets. Understanding and acknowledging the presence of risk is the first step towards developing a successful trading strategy.

1.2 Identifying Types of Risk

1.2.1 Market Risk: Market risk encompasses the uncertainties and fluctuations in the overall financial markets.
This includes factors such as economic conditions, political events, and market sentiment, which can impact the profitability of your trades.

Market risk refers to the potential losses resulting from changes in overall financial market conditions. It encompasses factors such as economic events, political developments, and market sentiment that can affect the profitability of trading activities.

Traders must analyze and assess market risk to make informed decisions and implement risk management strategies to mitigate potential losses.

Welcome to "Trading Insights: Your Path to Profitable Trading." In this book, we will explore the essential principles and strategies that will guide you towards success in the dynamic world of trading. Whether you're a beginner seeking a solid foundation or an experienced trader looking to refine your skills, this book provides practical insights to enhance your trading journey.

Trading is a captivating pursuit that requires a blend of knowledge, discipline, and adaptability. Throughout these pages, we will uncover key insights into market analysis, risk management, and trade execution. By understanding market behavior and employing effective risk management techniques, you will gain the confidence to make informed trading decisions.

Embracing a growth mindset and managing emotions are also vital aspects of successful trading. We will discuss techniques to foster a positive trading psychology, enabling you to navigate through challenges and maintain discipline in the face of market volatility.

Remember, success in trading is a continuous learning process. This book aims to equip you with the foundational tools and strategies to steer your trading journey towards profitability. Get ready to absorb valuable insights that will empower you to make smarter trades and unlock your potential as a profitable trader.

Are you ready to embark on this enlightening journey? Let's dive in, gain valuable "Trading Insights," and pave the way for a profitable trading future.

CONTENT OF THIS BOOK IS NOT FINANCIAL ADVICE

CONTENT LIST

Chapter 1: Mastering Risk Management for Trading Success

Chapter 2: Understanding Market Structure and Supply/Demand Zones

Chapter 3: The Power of Technical Analysis Tools and Indicators

Chapter 4: Building a Disciplined Trading Plan and Effective Trade Management Strategies

Chapter 5: Sustaining Motivation, Setting New Goals, and Embracing Personal Growth

For example, let's say you're a trader in the stock market. You have a portfolio of stocks, and you notice that there is increased uncertainty surrounding the economy due to a global economic downturn. This economic downturn leads to a decrease in consumer spending and a decline in corporate earnings.

As a result, the overall stock market experiences a significant downward trend. This is an example of market risk, as the broader market conditions are negatively impacting the value and performance of your stock portfolio.

To manage this market risk, you may consider implementing risk management techniques such as diversification by adding non-correlated assets to your portfolio. Additionally, you may use stop-loss orders to automatically sell your stocks if they reach a certain price level to limit potential losses.

By understanding market risk and implementing appropriate risk management strategies, traders can navigate uncertain market conditions with more confidence and minimize the impact of adverse market movements on their trading activities.

1.2.2 Liquidity risk: Refers to the potential difficulty or inability to execute trades promptly due to insufficient buyers or sellers in the market. It arises when there is a lack of liquidity, which can lead to delays, slippage, or challenges in exiting positions at desired prices. Understanding and managing liquidity risk is essential for traders, as it can impact the execution and profitability of their trades.

For example, let's say you are a trader in the stock market, and you decide to sell a large number of shares of a particular stock. However, you notice that there is a low volume of trading activity for that stock, indicating limited liquidity in the market.

As a result, when you attempt to sell your shares, only a small number of buyers are available, and there is not enough demand to absorb your sell order without significantly impacting the stock's price. Consequently, you may experience slippage, where your trade is executed at a lower price than anticipated due to the lack of liquidity in the market.

To manage liquidity risk in such situations, you may consider breaking down your sell order into smaller portions and executing them over a period of time to minimize the impact on market liquidity. Additionally, you could set limit orders at specific price levels that align with the market's liquidity conditions to ensure a more favorable execution.

1.2.3 Credit Risk

Refers to the potential for losses resulting from counterparty defaults or the inability of borrowers to fulfill their financial obligations. It arises when traders engage in transactions, such as margin trading or derivatives, where there is a reliance on the creditworthiness of the involved parties. Understanding and managing credit risk is essential for traders to protect their capital and mitigate potential losses.

For example, let's say you are a futures trader and enter into a futures contract with a counterparty. The contract specifies that the counterparty will deliver a certain commodity to you at a predetermined future date. However, as the delivery date approaches, you become aware that the counterparty is facing financial difficulties and may default on the contract. If the counterparty fails to fulfill their obligation, you may face credit risk, resulting in potential losses. A default could mean that you do not receive the commodity promised, and you may incur financial losses as a result.

To manage credit risk, traders should conduct thorough due diligence on their counterparties, assessing their creditworthiness and financial stability. Additionally, utilizing risk management tools such as collateral requirements or engaging in transactions through reputable clearinghouses can help mitigate potential credit risk.

1.2.4 Operational Risk

Operational risk is the potential for losses resulting from non-market factors that may impact trading outcomes. It encompasses risks associated with internal processes, systems, and external events that can disrupt trading activities. Understanding and managing operational risk is crucial for traders to ensure the smooth functioning of their operations and mitigate potential losses.

For example, let's say you are a day trader utilizing an online trading platform. During an active trading session, you encounter technical issues with the platform, preventing you from executing trades or accessing critical market information. These technical failures disrupt your trading activities and potentially result in missed trading opportunities or erroneous trade executions.

This scenario represents operational risk, where the efficiency and effectiveness of your trading activities are compromised due to operational issues.

To manage operational risk, traders should employ robust operational processes, including regular system checks, software updates, and utilizing reliable and secure trading platforms. Additionally, maintaining backups of critical data and having contingency plans in place can help minimize the impact of operational disruptions.

1.3 Measuring and Assessing Risk

1.3.1 Volatility: Volatility measures the variability and magnitude of price movements in financial instruments.
Understanding volatility is essential in determining potential risk and selecting appropriate risk management strategies.

Volatility refers to the degree of variability or fluctuations in the price of a financial instrument over a specific period.
It is a measure of market uncertainty and can have implications for trading decisions and risk management.
Understanding volatility and its impact is crucial for traders to assess potential risks and opportunities in the market.

For example, let's consider stock market volatility. If a particular stock experiences high volatility, it means that its price is fluctuating significantly within a given timeframe. This increased volatility could be due to various factors, such as earnings announcements, economic news, or market sentiment shifts.

As a trader, understanding the volatility of a stock allows you to gauge the potential risk and reward associated with trading that stock.
Higher volatility implies greater price swings, which can present both opportunities and increased risk. For instance, higher volatility may provide more significant profit potential but also carries the risk of larger losses if the market moves against your position.

To manage volatility risk, traders can use risk management techniques such as setting appropriate stop-loss orders to limit potential losses during volatile periods.
Additionally, employing trading strategies tailored to current market volatility levels, such as using volatility indicators or adjusting position sizes, can be beneficial.

By understanding volatility and considering its implications in trading decisions, traders can adapt their strategies, optimize risk management, and seize opportunities presented in volatile markets while mitigating potential losses.

1.3.2 Value at Risk (VaR):

VaR (Value at Risk) is a statistical technique used to estimate the potential losses within a certain level of confidence over a specified time horizon. It is a risk management tool that helps traders quantify and manage their exposure to market risk.

For example, suppose you have a trading portfolio with a value of $100,000. To calculate the VaR at a 95% confidence level, you estimate that the maximum potential loss within a one-day time horizon is $5,000. This means that there is a 5% chance of losing $5,000 or more in one trading day.

Using VaR, traders can assess their risk tolerance and set maximum risk limits. In this example, if the estimated VaR exceeds the trader's risk appetite, they may consider adjusting their positions, implementing risk mitigation strategies, or reducing the overall portfolio risk.

It's important to note that VaR is based on historical data and statistical models, and it assumes that market conditions will remain relatively stable. However, unexpected events or extreme market movements can exceed the estimated VaR.

1.3.3 Probability and Risk-Reward Ratio:

Probability and risk-reward ratio are crucial concepts in trading that help traders assess the potential outcomes of a trade and make informed decisions. Understanding these concepts assists in evaluating the risk and reward associated with each trade opportunity.

For example, let's consider a currency trader who believes that a particular currency pair will appreciate in value. Before entering the trade, the trader assesses the potential outcomes based on their analysis and assigns a probability to each outcome.

The trader estimates that there is a 70% chance of the currency pair moving in their favor and a 30% chance of it moving against them. Additionally, the trader establishes a risk-reward ratio for the trade, which means they identify the potential profit relative to the potential loss.

Suppose the trader determines that their trade will have a risk-reward ratio of 1:2, meaning they anticipate their potential profit to be twice the size of their potential loss if the trade goes as expected.

With this information, the trader can calculate the expected value of the trade.
Multiplying the probabilities with the respective outcomes (70% * 2 - 30% * 1), the trader determines that the expected value is positive, indicating a potentially profitable trade.

By considering probability and the risk-reward ratio, traders can assess the potential profitability and riskiness of a trade.
They can then make more informed decisions by only executing trades with favorable risk-reward ratios and higher probabilities of success.

It is important to note that probability and risk-reward ratios are subjective estimates based on the trader's analysis, and actual outcomes can deviate from these estimates.
Ongoing adjustment and refinement of these estimates are essential for effective trade decision-making.

1.4 Risk Management Techniques

1.4.1 Setting Stop-Loss Orders:

Setting stop-loss orders is a risk management technique that allows traders to define a predetermined price level at which their trade will be automatically closed, limiting potential losses. Stop-loss orders help traders protect their capital and manage risk effectively.

For example, let's say you are a stock trader and you purchase shares of Company X at $50 per share. However, you want to limit your potential losses in case the stock price goes down.

To protect your investment, you can set a stop-loss order at $45, five dollars below your entry price. If the stock price drops to or below $45, your stop-loss order will be triggered, and your shares will be sold automatically at the prevailing market price.
This ensures that your maximum potential loss per share is limited to $5.

By setting stop-loss orders, you can implement a risk management strategy that helps protect your capital from significant downturns in the market. It allows you to define your acceptable risk level beforehand, removing emotions from the decision-making process.

The specific placement of stop-loss orders may vary based on individual trading strategies, market conditions, and the level of risk tolerance. Traders need to consider factors such as support and resistance levels, volatility, and market trends when determining suitable stop-loss placement.

Remember, stop-loss orders are not foolproof, and there is still a possibility of slippage or unexpected market movements. Regular monitoring of trades and adjusting stop-loss levels as per market conditions or trade progress is recommended to ensure effective risk management.

Overall, setting stop-loss orders is a valuable technique for traders to limit losses, protect capital, and maintain discipline in their trading approach.

1.4.2 Position Sizing:

Position sizing is a risk management technique that involves determining the appropriate size or quantity of a trade based on the level of risk and the trader's account size. Proper position sizing helps traders manage risk effectively and optimize their portfolio performance.

For example, let's consider a forex trader with a trading account balance of $10,000. The trader follows a risk management strategy that limits their maximum risk exposure to 2% of their account balance on any given trade.

To calculate the position size, the trader would multiply their account balance ($10,000) by the risk percentage (2%), resulting in a maximum risk of $200 per trade.

Now, suppose the trader identifies a forex trade opportunity with a stop-loss level of 50 pips and determines that the acceptable risk per pip is $2. Dividing the maximum risk per trade ($200) by the risk per pip ($2), the trader determines that the position size should be 100,000 units of the currency pair (100,000 units x $0.02 per pip = $200).

By implementing proper position sizing, the trader ensures that each trade's risk is within their predefined risk tolerance level and aligns with their account size.
This approach helps control the impact of individual trades on the overall portfolio and avoids excessive exposure to potential losses.

It is crucial to adjust position sizes based on the volatility of the market, the specific trade setup, or any specific risk management rules set by the trader's strategy.
Regular assessment and adjustment of position sizes are necessary to adapt to changing market conditions and maintain effective risk management.

By incorporating position sizing techniques into their trading plan, traders can strike a balance between maximizing profit potential and managing risk, thus promoting the long-term sustainability of their trading activities.

1.4.3 Diversification:

Diversification is a risk management technique that involves spreading investments across different assets, markets, or instruments to reduce exposure to any single position or risk factor. It is a strategy used to minimize the impact of adverse events on the overall portfolio and potentially enhance risk-adjusted returns.

For example, let's consider an investor who has a portfolio consisting solely of stocks from the technology sector. If there is negative news specific to the technology sector, such as a product recall or a major cybersecurity breach, the value of the entire portfolio could be significantly affected.

To mitigate this risk, the investor decides to diversify their portfolio by including stocks from other sectors such as healthcare, finance, and consumer goods. By doing so, the investor is less reliant on the performance of a single sector and is better positioned to weather industry-specific shocks.

Diversification can extend beyond different sectors, including asset classes, geographies, or investment strategies. For instance, an investor may allocate some of their portfolio to bonds or real estate, thereby reducing the reliance on equities. Additionally, investing in international markets can provide exposure to different economies and currencies.

The goal of diversification is not to eliminate all risk, but rather to spread risk across a range of assets, which can result in a more stable and resilient portfolio. By diversifying, investors can potentially lower their overall portfolio volatility, smooth out returns, and potentially enhance risk-adjusted returns.

It's important to note that diversification should be based on thorough research and understanding of each investment. Furthermore, diversification does not guarantee profits or protect against losses, as all investments carry inherent risks. Regular monitoring and periodic rebalancing of the portfolio are essential to ensure the desired level of diversification is maintained.

By incorporating diversification into their investment strategy, investors can reduce their exposure to individual risks and increase the potential for long-term portfolio stability and success.

1.5 Emotional Discipline and Risk Management:

Emotional discipline plays a crucial role in effective risk management.
It involves managing and controlling emotions that can potentially cloud judgment and lead to impulsive or irrational decisions.
Here's a brief overview of emotional discipline and its connection to risk management:

1. Emotional Discipline:
Emotions like fear and greed can significantly impact our trading decisions.
Emotional discipline involves recognizing and managing these emotions to make rational and objective choices.

2. Maintaining Objectivity:
Practicing emotional discipline helps traders stay focused on their trading plan and long-term goals.
By keeping emotions in check, traders are better equipped to make rational decisions based on market analysis and risk management principles.

3. Avoiding Impulsive Behavior:

Emotional discipline helps traders avoid impulsive behaviors, such as chasing trades, overtrading, or deviating from their trading plan. It promotes patience and discipline in waiting for optimal setups to maximize potential returns.

4. Sticking to Risk Management Principles:

Emotional discipline is closely linked to implementing solid risk management techniques. Traders who maintain emotional discipline are more likely to adhere to stop-loss orders, employ proper position sizing, and effectively manage risk.

5. Controlling Stress and Anxiety:

Trading can be stressful, but emotional discipline helps traders manage stress and anxiety levels. By practicing techniques like deep breathing, mindfulness, and maintaining a healthy work-life balance, traders can approach the markets with a clear and focused mindset.

Remember, emotional discipline is an ongoing process that requires self-awareness, practice, and continuous improvement. By cultivating emotional discipline in conjunction with sound risk management principles, traders enhance their ability to make rational decisions and achieve long-term success.

Conclusion

Understanding risk and implementing effective risk management techniques are vital steps on your trading journey.

By comprehending the various types of risk that exist, measuring and assessing risk, and adopting appropriate risk management strategies, you can protect your capital and increase your odds of trading success.

In the subsequent sections of this book, we will explore additional risk management techniques and delve into the psychological aspect of trading, discussing how emotions can impact decision-making.

Ultimately, mastering risk management is a key pillar in achieving sustainable profitability and longevity in the trading world.

Chapter 2: Understanding Market Structure and Supply/Demand Zones

2.1: Market Structure: The Building Blocks of Price Movements

In this section, we will delve into the concept of market structure and its significance in understanding price movements.

Market structure provides the foundation for technical analysis and helps traders identify trends, support and resistance levels, and potential trading opportunities.

Understanding market structure is essential for making informed trading decisions.

2.1.1 Definition of Market Structure:

Market structure refers to the overall characteristics and organization of a financial market. It provides insights into the behavior of market participants, the underlying supply and demand forces, and the dynamics influencing price movements. Understanding market structure is essential for analyzing trends, identifying support and resistance levels, and making informed trading decisions.

For example, let's consider the stock market. The market structure can be defined as the collective arrangement of buyers and sellers, market participants' behavior, and the organization of trading activities for stocks. It encompasses factors such as liquidity, trading volume, bid-ask spread, and market depth.

Market structure analysis involves examining various elements, including price patterns, trends, volume, and market participant activities, to gain a comprehensive understanding of how the market is functioning. Traders analyze charts and indicators to identify the market structure and determine potential trading opportunities.

For instance, if an uptrend is evident in a stock's price chart, with higher highs and higher lows, this suggests a bullish market structure. This information can guide traders to look for buying opportunities or ride the upward momentum. On the other hand, a series of lower highs and lower lows indicate a downtrend and a bearish market structure, signaling potential selling or shorting opportunities.

Market structure analysis also involves identifying support and resistance levels. These are price levels at which buying or selling pressure is expected to be significant, potentially causing the price to reverse or consolidate. Traders use support and resistance levels to plan their entry and exit points or to adjust stop-loss orders.

Understanding market structure helps traders anticipate the behavior of market participants, identify trends, and detect potential price reversals or continuation patterns. By analyzing market structure, traders can make more informed trading decisions and develop effective strategies to capitalize on market opportunities.

It is important to note that market structure is dynamic and can change over time. Therefore, ongoing analysis and regular monitoring of market structure are necessary to adapt to evolving market conditions and maximize trading potential.

2.1.2 Trend Analysis:

Trend analysis is a method used to identify and analyze the overall direction of price movements in a financial market. It helps traders gain insights into the prevailing market sentiment and make informed trading decisions. Understanding and analyzing trends is crucial for identifying potential entry and exit points in trades.

For example, let's consider the price of a stock over a specific time period. By analyzing the stock's price chart, a trader notices a consistent pattern of higher highs and higher lows. This indicates an uptrend in the stock's price.

The trader can use trend analysis to guide their trading decisions. They may look for opportunities to enter the market by buying the stock when it experiences temporary price pullbacks or consolidations within the overall upward trend. They may also consider setting profit targets or trailing stop-loss orders to capture potential gains if the trend continues.

Conversely, if the price chart shows a consistent pattern of lower highs and lower lows, it indicates a downtrend. In this scenario, traders may consider short-selling the stock or entering trades that align with the downward price movement.

Trend analysis can be applied to various timeframes, ranging from short-term intraday trends to longer-term trends spanning weeks, months, or even years. Traders often use different technical indicators or chart patterns to confirm and validate trends before making trading decisions.

By conducting trend analysis, traders can align their trades with the prevailing market direction, increasing the probability of successful trades. However, it's essential to keep in mind that trends can change or reverse abruptly, so regular monitoring and reassessment of trend analysis are necessary for effective trading.

.

Trend analysis is a valuable tool for traders to navigate the market and make informed decisions based on the prevailing price movements. By identifying and analyzing trends, traders can adapt their strategies to capitalize on market opportunities and avoid potential setbacks in their trading activities

2.1.3 Support and Resistance:

Support and resistance levels are key components of technical analysis used by traders to identify potential levels at which buying or selling pressure may emerge, causing the price of a financial instrument to reverse or consolidate.
Understanding support and resistance levels helps traders make informed decisions about entry and exit points, as well as risk management strategies.

For example, let's consider a stock that has been steadily increasing in price. As the price continues to rise, it reaches a specific level where it encounters selling pressure, causing the price to stop its upward movement and reverse. This level, where the selling pressure overwhelms the buying pressure, is called a resistance level.

Once the price retreats from the resistance level, it may eventually find a floor, a level where buying interest exceeds selling pressure, leading to a price rebound. This level, where the buying pressure outweighs the selling pressure, is called a support level.

Traders use support and resistance levels to make trading decisions. When the price approaches a support level, traders may see it as a buying opportunity since support represents a potential price floor. They may consider opening new positions or placing stop-buy orders near the support level to capture potential price gains.

On the other hand, when the price approaches a resistance level, traders may see it as a selling opportunity since resistance represents a potential price ceiling. They may consider closing existing positions or placing stop-sell orders near the resistance level to lock in profits.
Support and resistance levels can be identified through various technical analysis tools, such as trendlines, moving averages, chart patterns, or previous price swing highs and lows. The more times a level is tested and holds, the stronger it is considered to be.

It's important to note that support and resistance levels are not exact price points, but rather zones or areas where there is a higher probability of price reactions. The effectiveness of support and resistance levels can vary based on market conditions and the strength of the trend.

By identifying and monitoring support and resistance levels, traders can improve their market timing, set appropriate entry and exit points, and incorporate risk management strategies in their trading plans. Recognizing and acting upon these key levels can enhance the likelihood of successful trades and help protect against potential losses.

2.1.4 Price Patterns:

Price patterns are repetitive formations that appear on price charts and provide insights into market psychology and potential future price movements. Traders analyze these patterns to identify potential trading opportunities, predict trend reversals or continuations, and make informed trading decisions.

There are several commonly observed price patterns, including:

a. Double Tops and Bottoms: These patterns occur when the price attempts to break a previous high (double top) or low (double bottom) but fails, creating a reversal signal.

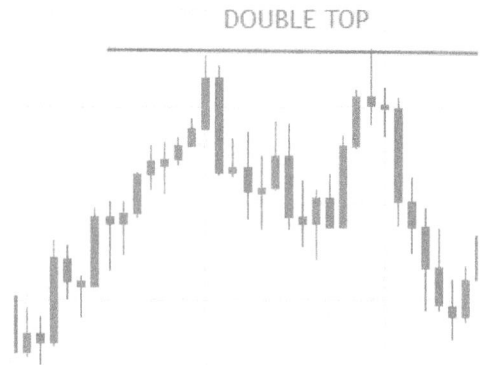

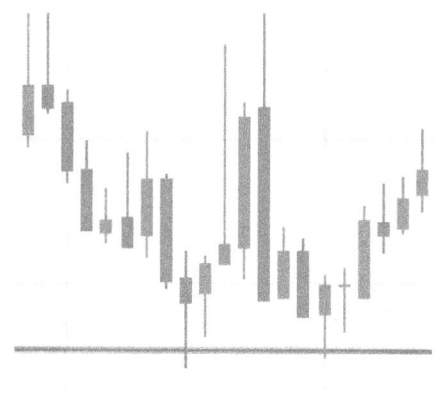

b. Triangles: Triangles are formed by converging trend lines, indicating a period of consolidation before an eventual breakout in price.

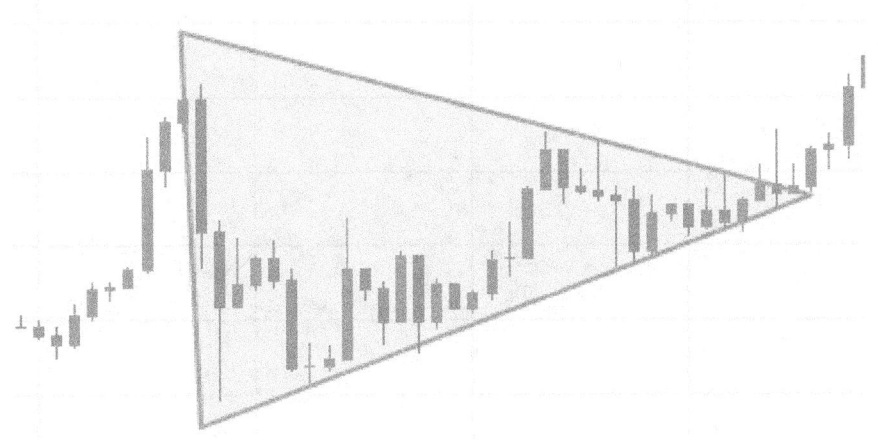

c. Head and Shoulders: This pattern resembles a head and two shoulders and indicates a potential trend reversal from bullish to bearish (head and shoulders top) or from bearish to bullish (head and shoulders bottom).

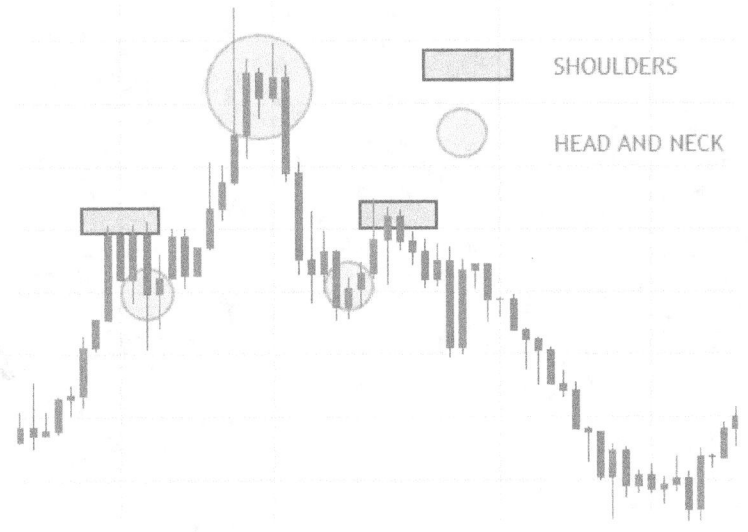

d. Wedges: Wedges are characterized by converging trend lines that slope in the same direction, indicating a potential reversal or continuation of an existing trend.

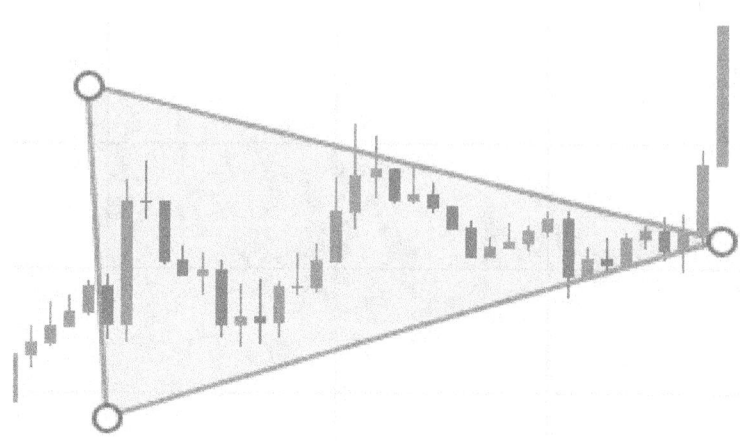

e. Flags and Pennants: Flags and pennants are short-term continuation patterns that represent a temporary pause in the price movement before the trend resumes.

f. Cup and Handle: This pattern resembles a cup with a handle and is considered a bullish continuation pattern.

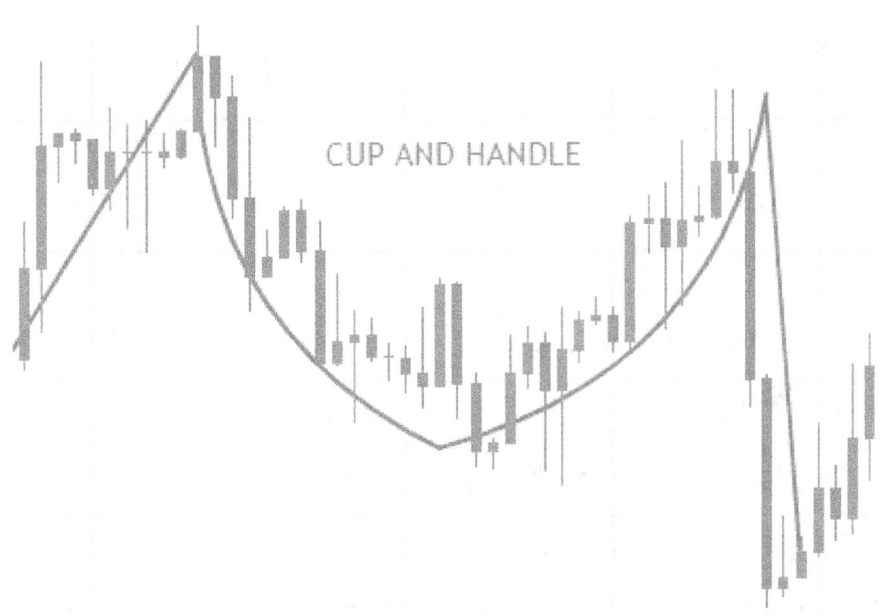

Traders analyze these price patterns to determine the market sentiment and anticipate future price movements. They look for confirmation signals, such as breakouts or breakdowns above or below pattern boundaries, to enter trades or adjust existing positions.

It is important to note that price patterns are not foolproof indicators and should be used in conjunction with other technical analysis tools and risk management strategies.
Traders must be aware of false signals and consider factors such as volume, trend strength, and overall market conditions while interpreting price patterns.

Additionally, price patterns can occur on various timeframes, from intraday charts to weekly or monthly charts.
Traders may choose to focus on specific timeframes based on their trading strategies and objectives.

By recognizing and understanding price patterns, traders can enhance their ability to identify potential trading opportunities and anticipate upcoming price movements.
Regular monitoring of price patterns and their reliability in specific market conditions can contribute to more successful trading outcomes.

2.1.5 Market Participants and Order Flow

Understanding market participants and their behavior is another aspect of market structure analysis.
Traders analyze order flow, volume, and liquidity levels to gauge market sentiment and potential price reversals.
Monitoring the actions of institutional investors, market makers, and retail traders contributes to a comprehensive understanding of market structure.

2.2.1 Supply and Demand Zones:

Supply and demand zones are areas on a price chart where significant buying or selling interest has been previously observed.
They represent levels where the balance between supply and demand has shifted, potentially influencing future price movements.
Understanding supply and demand zones is crucial for identifying potential areas of support and resistance and making informed trading decisions.

1. Supply Zone:

A supply zone, also known as a resistance zone, is an area on a price chart where selling pressure exceeds buying pressure, potentially halting or reversing the upward price movement. It is a level where sellers are more likely to enter the market, leading to a potential price decrease.

Example: In a stock that has been increasing in price, a supply zone can be observed when the price reaches a specific level where the market consistently experiences selling pressure. Traders may perceive this zone as an opportunity to sell or short the stock, expecting a potential price reversal or pullback.

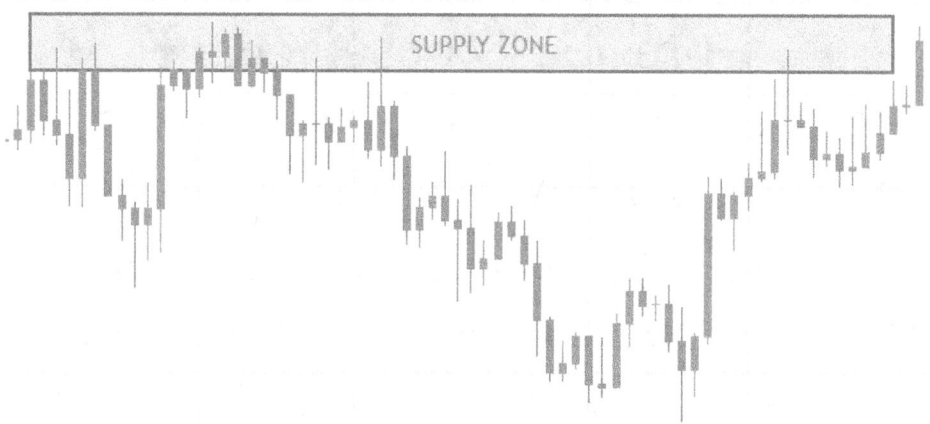

2. Demand Zone:

A demand zone, also known as a support zone, is an area on a price chart where buying interest exceeds selling pressure, potentially halting or reversing the downward price movement. It is a level where buyers are more likely to enter the market, leading to a potential price increase.

Example: In a currency pair that has been declining in value, a demand zone can be observed when the price reaches a specific level where the market consistently experiences buying interest. Traders may perceive this zone as an opportunity to buy the currency pair, expecting a potential price reversal or bounce.

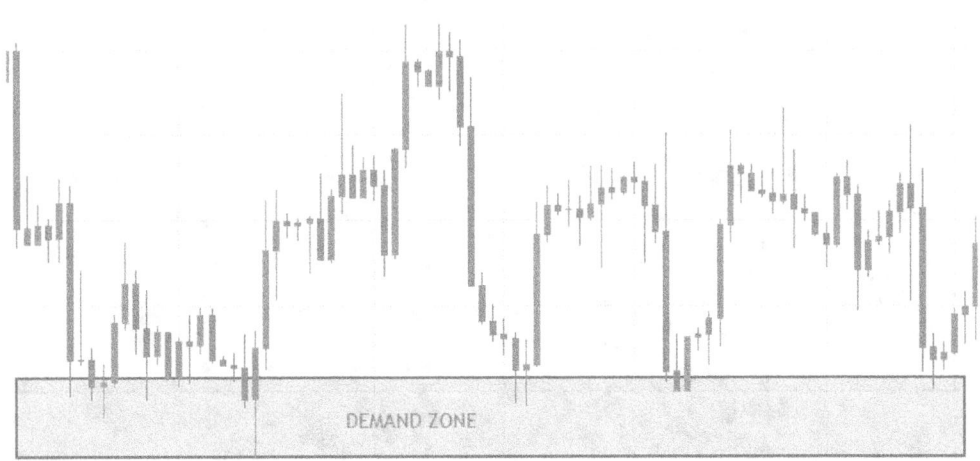

3. Flip Zone:

A flip zone occurs when a previous resistance zone turns into a support zone or vice versa. It represents a significant shift in market sentiment and can provide trading opportunities.

Example: Let's consider a stock that has previously encountered selling pressure at a specific price level, forming a supply zone. However, in a subsequent price decline, the stock reaches that same level but now shows buying interest, indicating a shift from a supply zone to a demand zone. Traders may view this flip zone as a potential area of support where the stock could reverse its downtrend and present a buying opportunity.

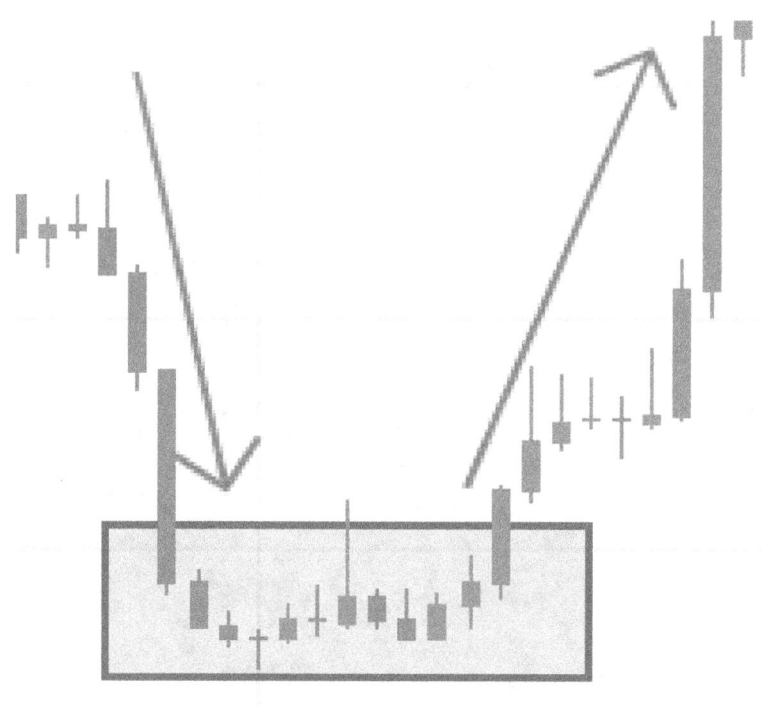

FLIP ZONE

Traders use supply and demand zones to make trading decisions, such as determining entry and exit points, setting profit targets or stop-loss levels, and identifying potential price reversals or continuations.

These zones can be identified using various techniques, such as analyzing historic price levels, volume profiles, or using specific technical analysis tools.

It's important to note that supply and demand zones should not be considered as precise levels but rather as zones with a higher probability of price reactions.

Traders should also consider other factors such as market context, trend analysis, and volume confirmation to complement their supply and demand zone analysis.

2.2.2. Trading Opportunities with Supply and Demand Zones:

Supply and demand zones provide traders with valuable trading opportunities, as they represent areas on a price chart where significant buying or selling pressure has occurred in the past.

Traders can utilize supply and demand zones to identify potential areas of support and resistance and make informed trading decisions.

For example, consider a stock that has been in an uptrend, but encounters a supply zone where selling pressure is expected to outweigh buying interest.

As the price approaches the supply zone, traders may look for specific trading opportunities:

a. Short Selling: Traders who anticipate a potential price reversal from the supply zone may initiate short selling positions.

They would borrow shares of the stock from a broker, sell them at the prevailing market price, and aim to buy them back at a lower price when the stock price declines.

By profiting from the decrease in price, traders can take advantage of the expected selling pressure in the supply zone.

b. Exiting Long Positions: Traders who are holding long positions in the stock may consider exiting their positions or taking partial profits near the supply zone.

This enables them to lock in gains before the potential price reversal or pullback occurs.

Conversely, in a downtrending market, traders may look for potential trading opportunities when price reaches a demand zone:

a. Buying Opportunities: Traders who anticipate a potential price reversal from the demand zone may initiate long positions. They would buy the stock at the prevailing market price with the expectation that buying interest and support found in the demand zone will lead to a price increase or trend reversal.

b. Exiting Short Positions: Traders who have short positions in the stock may consider exiting their positions or taking partial profits near the demand zone. This allows them to secure profits before the potential price rally or bounce occurs.

It's important to note that trading opportunities with supply and demand zones should be confirmed by other technical indicators or price action analysis. Traders should also consider the broader market context, overall trend, and volume confirmation before executing trades.

By effectively identifying and utilizing supply and demand zones, traders can enhance their ability to spot potential areas of support and resistance.

2.2.3. Risk Management and Supply/Demand Zone Analysis:

Supply and demand zone analysis can play a crucial role in coordinating effective risk management strategies for traders.
By incorporating supply and demand zones into their risk management approach, traders can better determine entry and exit points, set appropriate stop-loss levels, and adjust their position sizes based on market dynamics.

Here's an example of how supply and demand zones can be used to coordinate risk management:

Suppose a trader is analyzing the price chart of a currency pair and identifies a strong supply zone near a significant resistance level.
The trader believes that the price is likely to reverse from this zone and potentially trend downwards.

To coordinate their risk management:

1. Entry Point: The trader decides to enter a short position near the supply zone, aiming to benefit from a potential price decline. By entering near the supply zone, the trader is positioning themselves to capture potential profits if the anticipated price reversal occurs.

2. Stop-loss Placement: To manage potential losses in case the price breaks above the supply zone, the trader sets a stop-loss order just above the supply zone. This way, if the price moves against their position and breaks out of the zone, the stop-loss order will be triggered, helping to limit the trader's potential losses.

3. Position Sizing: The trader adjusts their position size based on the strength and reliability of the supply zone. If the supply zone is considered strong and has been tested multiple times, indicating a higher probability of a successful trade, the trader may decide to allocate a larger position size with a corresponding increase in potential profit. On the other hand, if the supply zone is less established or has less confidence, the trader may opt for a smaller position size to minimize potential losses.

By incorporating risk management principles into the supply and demand zone analysis, the trader is effectively managing their potential risk exposure. They are entering the trade at a strategically chosen level, setting a stop-loss order to control losses if the price does not behave as expected, and adjusting their position size to align with the strength of the supply zone.

It is important for traders to conduct thorough analysis, regularly reassess supply and demand zones, and adapt their risk management strategies to changing market conditions. By effectively coordinating risk management with supply and demand zone analysis, traders can optimize their risk-reward ratios and increase the probability of successful trades.

Conclusion

Market structure is a fundamental concept in understanding price movements and identifying trading opportunities. By analyzing trends, support and resistance levels, price patterns, and market participant behavior, traders can gain valuable insights into the dynamics of a financial market. Understanding market structure sets the stage for more advanced technical analysis techniques and effective trading strategies

Chapter 3: The Power of Technical Analysis Tools and Indicators

Introduction to Technical Analysis Tools and Indicators

In this section, we will delve into the power of technical analysis tools and indicators and their significance in analyzing and predicting price movements. Technical analysis tools and indicators assist traders in making informed decisions by analyzing historical price data, volume, and other market statistics. They provide valuable insights into market trends, patterns, and potential trading opportunities.

3.1 Understanding Technical Analysis Tools and Indicators

Technical analysis tools and indicators are mathematical calculations or visual representations of market data that aid in interpreting price patterns and trends. They help traders analyze price movements, identify potential entry and exit points, and determine risk management strategies. These tools and indicators can be applied to various timeframes and financial instruments.

3.2 Advantages of Technical Analysis Tools and Indicators

There are several advantages to using technical analysis tools and indicators:

a. Objective Analysis: Technical analysis tools provide objective data derived from historical price and volume information, helping traders make logical decisions based on data rather than emotions or subjective opinions.

b. Timing Entry and Exit Points: By analyzing price patterns and indicators, traders can identify potential entry and exit points for trades. This enhances timing and increases the likelihood of profitable trades.

c. Risk Management: Technical analysis tools assist in setting appropriate stop-loss levels and managing risk. They help traders determine optimal positions to protect against potential losses.

d. Confirmation of Patterns: Indicators act as confirmation tools, verifying the validity of chart patterns. This increases the reliability of trading signals and reduces the likelihood of false breakouts or trend reversals.

3.3 Common Technical Analysis Tools and Indicators

There is a wide range of technical analysis tools and indicators available, each serving specific purposes. Some commonly used ones include:

3.3.1 Moving Averages:

Moving averages are one of the most widely used technical analysis tools.
They help traders identify trends, smooth out price fluctuations, and generate potential entry and exit signals.
A moving average calculates the average price of an asset over a specific period, updating with each new data point.

There are different types of moving averages, including the simple moving average (SMA) and the exponential moving average (EMA).
The SMA gives equal weight to each data point in the calculation, while the EMA assigns more weight to recent data, making it more responsive to current price changes.

Let's consider an example to understand how moving averages are applied:

Suppose a trader is analyzing the daily price chart of a stock over the past 50 days. They decide to use a simple moving average (SMA) with a period of 20 days to identify potential trends and trading signals.

1. Identifying Trends:

The trader plots the 20-day SMA on the chart, which connects the average price of the stock over the past 20 days. By observing the price in relation to the moving average, the trader can identify the direction of the trend.

If the price is consistently above the moving average, it indicates an uptrend. Conversely, if the price is consistently below the moving average, it suggests a downtrend. Changes in the slope or crossover of moving averages of different periods can also indicate potential trend reversals.

2. Generating Trading Signals:

Moving averages can also generate trading signals when a shorter-term moving average crosses above or below a longer-term moving average.

For example, if the 20-day SMA crosses above the 50-day SMA, it is known as a "golden cross" and often signals a bullish trend. Traders may interpret this crossover as a buying opportunity.

Conversely, if the 20-day SMA crosses below the 50-day SMA, it is called a "death cross" and typically indicates a bearish trend. Traders may interpret this crossover as a selling opportunity or a signal to short the asset.

3. Support and Resistance Levels:

Moving averages can also act as support or resistance levels. In an uptrend, the moving average may provide support, with the price bouncing off the average during pullbacks. In a downtrend, the moving average may act as a resistance level, with the price finding difficulty in breaking above it.

Traders may use the moving average as a reference point to set stop-loss orders or determine profit targets.

It's important to note that moving averages work best in trending markets and may generate false signals during periods of consolidation or sideways movement. Therefore, it's recommended to use moving averages in combination with other technical indicators and analysis tools for confirmation.

By applying moving averages effectively, traders can identify trends, generate trading signals, and adjust their strategies based on market conditions. Each trader may choose different periods for their moving averages based on their trading style, timeframes, and asset being analyzed.

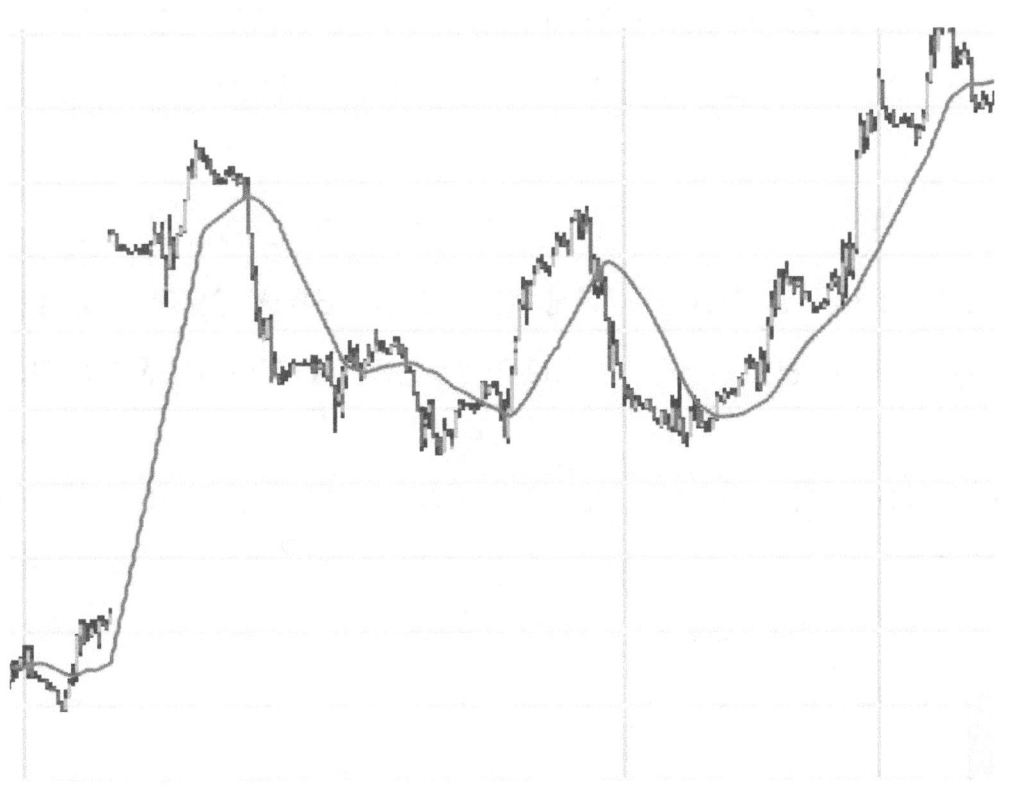

3.3.2. Relative Strength Index (RSI):

The Relative Strength Index (RSI) is a popular momentum indicator used in technical analysis to assess overbought and oversold conditions of an asset.

It measures the speed and magnitude of price movements, providing traders with potential signals for trend reversals or continuations.

The RSI is typically displayed as an oscillator that fluctuates between 0 and 100.

Let's explore how the RSI works and consider an example to see it in action:

1. Calculation and Interpretation:

The RSI calculates the ratio of average gains to average losses over a specified period, typically 14 days.

The formula normalizes the result to a value between 0 and 100.

- RSI values above 70 are commonly interpreted as indicating an overbought condition, suggesting that the asset may be due for a price correction or reversal. It implies that buying pressure may have pushed the price too high, and a pullback could occur.
- RSI values below 30 are generally seen as indicating an oversold condition, suggesting that the asset may be undervalued or due for a bounce. It implies that selling pressure may have pushed the price too low, and a potential price rebound could occur.

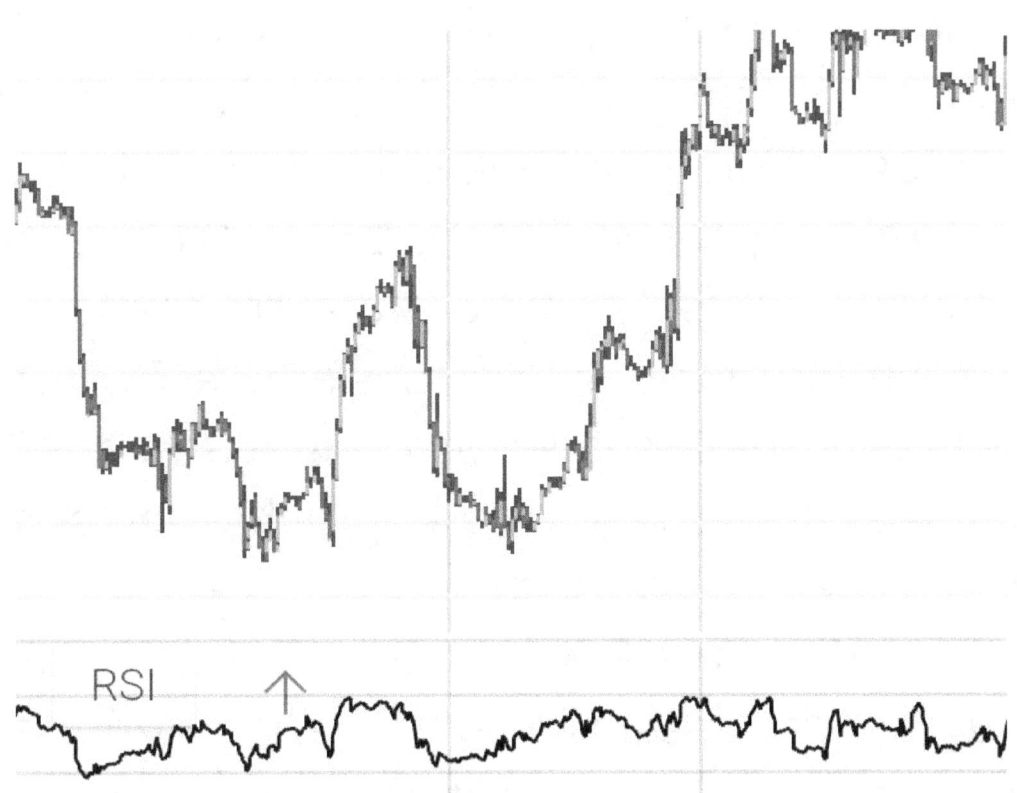

2. Generating Trading Signals:

Traders often look for specific signals on the RSI chart to generate trading decisions. Some commonly used techniques include:

- Divergence: Divergence occurs when the price of an asset moves in the opposite direction of the RSI. Bullish divergence is observed when the price makes lower lows while the RSI makes higher lows, indicating a potential bullish reversal. Conversely, bearish divergence is seen when the price makes higher highs while the RSI makes lower highs, suggesting a potential bearish reversal.
- Overbought/Oversold Levels: Traders watch for RSI values crossing above 70 (overbought) or below 30 (oversold) to signal potential reversals.

For example, if the RSI crosses above 70, it may indicate that the asset is overbought and due for a price correction, suggesting a possible sell or short opportunity.

Conversely, if the RSI crosses below 30, it may indicate that the asset is oversold and due for a price bounce, suggesting a potential buying opportunity.

3. Example:

Suppose a trader is analyzing the daily price chart of a stock and observes the RSI to assess overbought or oversold conditions.

If the RSI value is above 70, indicating overbought conditions, and the stock is showing bearish divergence (price making higher highs while RSI making lower highs), the trader may interpret this as a potential signal for a bearish reversal. They might consider initiating a short position or tightening stop-loss levels on existing long positions.

Conversely, if the RSI value is below 30, indicating oversold conditions, and the stock is showing bullish divergence (price making lower lows while RSI making higher lows), the trader may interpret this as a potential signal for a bullish reversal. They might consider initiating a long position or tightening stop-loss levels on existing short positions.

It's important to note that the RSI is just one tool among many and should be used in conjunction with other technical analysis tools and indicators for confirmation. Additionally, market conditions and the overall trend should be considered when interpreting RSI signals.

3.3.3 Bollinger Bands:

Bollinger Bands are a widely used technical analysis tool designed to measure volatility and identify potential price breakouts or reversals. Created by John Bollinger, these bands consist of three lines plotted on a price chart: a middle band (usually a 20-day simple moving average) and an upper and lower band that are typically two standard deviations away from the middle band.

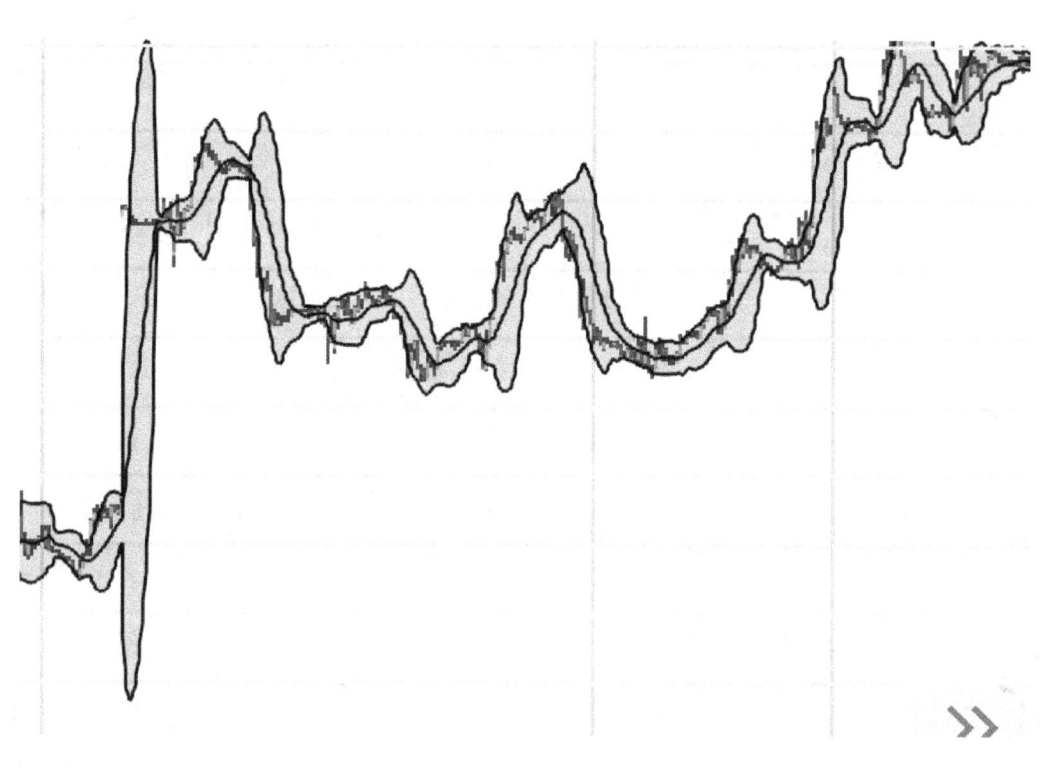

Let's explore how Bollinger Bands work and consider an example to see them in action:

1. Calculation and Interpretation:
Bollinger Bands are based on statistical calculations using standard deviation to gauge price volatility. The standard settings use a 20-day moving average and a standard deviation of two.

The middle band represents the average price over a specific period, typically a 20-day simple moving average.
The upper and lower bands are calculated by adding and subtracting a multiple of the standard deviation from the middle band.

As the price moves within the bands, it is considered within a normal trading range.
When the price reaches the upper band, it indicates potential overbought conditions, while reaching the lower band suggests possible oversold conditions.

2. Volatility and Breakouts:

Bollinger Bands provide insights into market volatility. During periods of low volatility, the bands contract, indicating a range-bound market.

Conversely, when volatility increases, the bands expand, signaling potential breakouts or larger price moves.

A breakout above the upper band suggests bullish momentum and a potential upward price continuation.
Traders may interpret this as a buying opportunity or a signal to continue holding long positions.

A breakout below the lower band indicates bearish momentum and a potential downward price continuation.
Traders may perceive this as a selling opportunity or a signal to maintain short positions or tighten stop-loss levels.

Example:

Suppose a trader is analyzing the daily price chart of a stock using Bollinger Bands.

If the stock's price is consistently reaching or exceeding the upper band, and the bands are expanding, it may indicate a period of strong bullish momentum. This suggests that the stock is overbought and due for a potential pullback. Traders may consider selling or shorting the stock, anticipating a price correction.

Conversely, if the price consistently approaches or falls below the lower band, and the bands are expanding, it may indicate a period of strong bearish momentum. This suggests that the stock is oversold and may be due for a potential bounce or reversal. Traders may consider buying the stock, expecting a price rebound.

It's important to note that Bollinger Bands are not standalone trading signals and should be used in conjunction with other technical analysis tools and indicators for confirmation. Market conditions, trend analysis, and additional technical factors should also be considered.

3.3.4 Fibonacci Retracement:

Fibonacci retracement is a popular technical analysis tool used to identify potential support and resistance levels in a price chart. It is based on the principle of retracement, where the price of an asset temporarily reverses direction before continuing in the original trend. Fibonacci retracement levels are derived from the Fibonacci sequence of numbers and are widely used by traders to identify areas of potential price reversals and continuation.

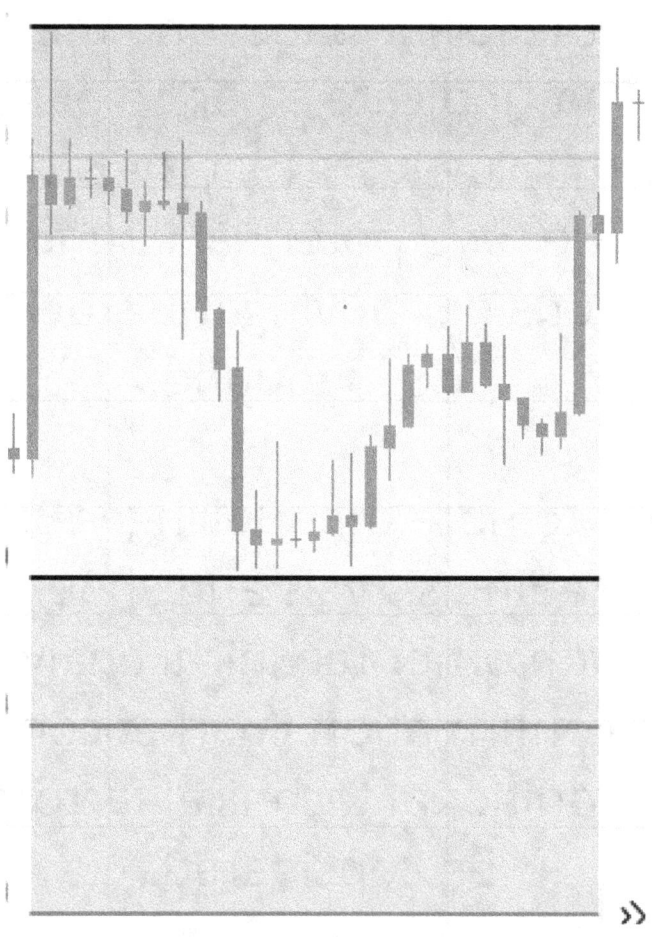

Let's explore how Fibonacci retracement works and consider an example to see it in action:

1. Determining Fibonacci Retracement Levels:

To apply Fibonacci retracement, traders identify a significant price swing or trend (usually identified as a swing high and swing low) and then draw the retracement levels.
Common retracement levels are 23.6%, 38.2%, 50%, 61.8%, and 78.6%.

The 0% level represents the starting point of the price swing (swing low), and the 100% level indicates the ending point (swing high).

2. Interpretation and Trading Decisions:

Fibonacci retracement levels act as potential support or resistance zones.

Here's how traders interpret these levels:

- If the price retraces to one of the Fibonacci levels, traders may anticipate a reversal or a bounce from that level and consider it as a potential buying or selling opportunity.

The key Fibonacci retracement levels to watch for potential reversals are the 38.2%, 50%, and 61.8% levels.

If the price holds these levels and resumes the original trend, it confirms the strength of the trend.
- Additionally, the 23.6% and 78.6% levels are often used as potential support or resistance areas.

If the price retraces to these levels and holds, traders may anticipate a continuation of the trend.

Example:

Suppose a trader is analyzing the price chart of a currency pair and identifies an uptrend. The trader then determines a swing high and swing low, and applies Fibonacci retracement levels to assess potential support and resistance areas.

If the price begins to retrace and reaches the 61.8% Fibonacci retracement level, the trader may anticipate a potential bounce from that level. If the price holds the 61.8% retracement level and resumes its upward movement, it suggests that the uptrend is still intact and provides a potential buying opportunity.

Conversely, if the price retraces further and falls below the 61.8% retracement level, it may indicate a potential trend reversal or a deeper correction. Traders may consider adjusting their trading strategy accordingly, such as taking profits on long positions or even considering short positions.

It's important to note that Fibonacci retracement levels should be used in conjunction with other technical analysis tools, such as trend lines, moving averages, or oscillators, to confirm potential reversals or continuations.

Additionally, Fibonacci retracement is a subjective tool and different traders may draw retracement levels differently based on their interpretation of significant price swings.

By effectively utilizing Fibonacci retracement, traders can identify potential areas of support and resistance, anticipate price reversals or continuations, and make informed trading decisions.

However, it is always advised to consider market context, other technical factors, and risk management strategies when incorporating Fibonacci retracement into a trading plan.

3.3.5 MACD (Moving Average Convergence Divergence):

The Moving Average Convergence Divergence (MACD) is a popular technical analysis indicator that measures momentum and provides insights into potential trend reversals and continuations.

It consists of two lines plotted on a chart: the MACD line and the signal line.
Additionally, the MACD histogram visualizes the difference between these two lines.

Let's explore how MACD works and consider an example to see it in action:

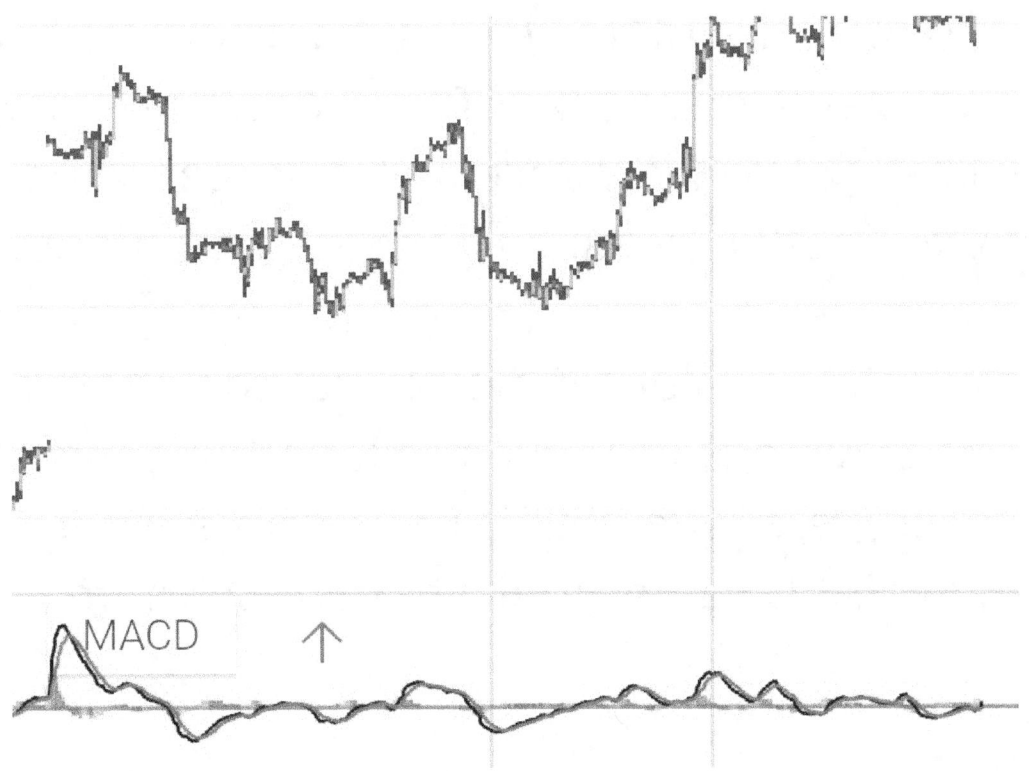

1. Calculation and Interpretation:

The MACD is calculated by subtracting a long-term exponential moving average (typically a 26-day EMA) from a short-term exponential moving average (typically a 12-day EMA).
The resulting MACD line represents the difference between these two moving averages.

The signal line is usually a 9-day EMA of the MACD line. It serves as a trigger line for potential buy or sell signals.

Additionally, the MACD histogram represents the difference between the MACD line and the signal line. It visualizes the convergence and divergence between the two lines, indicating changes in momentum.

Positive MACD values indicate that the short-term moving average is above the long-term moving average, suggesting bullish momentum.
Negative MACD values indicate bearish momentum.

2. Generating Trading Signals:

Traders analyze the MACD line, signal line crossover, and the MACD histogram to generate trading signals. Here are a few commonly used techniques:

- MACD Line and Signal Line Crossover: When the MACD line crosses above the signal line, it generates a bullish signal, suggesting that it may be an opportune time to buy or enter a long position. Conversely, when the MACD line crosses below the signal line, it generates a bearish signal, indicating a potential selling or shorting opportunity.

- Divergence: MACD divergence occurs when the price trend diverges from the MACD line.
Bullish divergence is observed when the price makes lower lows while the MACD line makes higher lows, indicating a potential bullish reversal.
Conversely, bearish divergence is seen when the price makes higher highs while the MACD line makes lower highs, suggesting a potential bearish reversal.

Example:

Suppose a trader is analyzing the daily price chart of a stock and using MACD to assess momentum and potential trading opportunities.

If the MACD line crosses above the signal line from below, it generates a bullish signal. Traders may consider initiating long positions or tightening stop-loss levels on existing short positions, anticipating a potential price increase.

Conversely, if the MACD line crosses below the signal line from above, it generates a bearish signal. Traders may consider selling or shorting the stock, expecting a potential price decrease.

The MACD histogram also provides valuable information about momentum. When the histogram is positive and increases in height, it indicates increasing bullish momentum. Conversely, when the histogram is negative and decreases in height, it suggests increasing bearish momentum.

It's important to note that MACD should be used in conjunction with other technical analysis tools and indicators to confirm potential trading signals. Additionally, considering market conditions, trend analysis, and other technical factors is essential for effective decision-making.

By incorporating MACD into their analysis, traders can gain insights into momentum and potential trend reversals or continuations.
This information can assist in making informed trading decisions and managing positions in the market.

Limitations of Technical Analysis Tools and Indicators

While technical analysis tools and indicators provide valuable insights, it is important to recognize their limitations.
Market conditions, unexpected news events, or shifts in market sentiment can lead to price movements that cannot be fully predicted by technical indicators alone.
Therefore, it is crucial to incorporate risk management measures and consider other fundamental or macroeconomic factors.

Chapter 4: Building a Disciplined Trading Plan and Effective Trade Management Strategies

Introduction to Building a Trading Plan

In this section, we will explore the importance of having a disciplined trading plan and effective trade management strategies.
A trading plan outlines a trader's approach to the market, defines their goals and risk tolerance, and provides a framework for decision-making.

Trade management strategies help traders effectively manage their trades, control risk, and optimize profitability.

4.1 Why Build a Trading Plan?

A trading plan is essential for consistent and disciplined trading. It helps traders stay focused, make objective decisions, and avoid impulsive or emotional trading. Key benefits of having a trading plan include:

- Clear Objectives: A trading plan helps define specific trading goals, such as profit targets, risk limits, and desired market exposure. It provides a roadmap for achieving these objectives.
- Risk Management: A trading plan includes risk management strategies, such as setting stop-loss orders, position sizes, and risk-reward ratios. It helps protect against excessive losses and ensures prudent risk control.
- Consistency: Following a trading plan promotes consistency in trading decisions, reducing the impact of emotional biases and increasing the probability of long-term success.
- Adaptability: A trading plan should be adaptable to market conditions and allow for adjustments as needed. This flexibility helps traders navigate changing market dynamics and avoid rigid decision-making.

4.2: Components of a Trading Plan

A well-structured trading plan typically includes the following components:

4.2.1 Trading Goals:

Trading goals are the specific objectives that traders set for themselves to guide their trading activities and measure their progress.

These goals help provide clarity and direction, aligning trading decisions with desired outcomes.

Setting realistic and specific trading goals is crucial for success in the markets.

Let's explore how trading goals work and consider an example to understand their importance:

1. Importance of Trading Goals:

Having clear trading goals serves several purposes:

- Focus and Motivation:

Goals provide a clear focus and purpose for a trader. They act as a driving force, keeping traders motivated and committed to their trading activities.

- Measure of Progress:

Goals provide a benchmark to assess performance and progress.

Traders can track their results against their set goals to determine if they are on track or need adjustments in their trading approach.

- Decision-making Framework:

Goals help guide trading decisions.

When faced with multiple opportunities or market conditions, traders can analyze whether a trade aligns with their goals and risk tolerance before making a decision.

2. Types of Trading Goals:

Trading goals can vary depending on an individual's trading style, risk appetite, and preferences. Here are some common types of trading goals:

- Profitability Goals:
These goals revolve around generating consistent profits from trading activities. Traders may set targets for daily, weekly, monthly, or annual profits based on their risk appetite and trading strategies.

- Risk Management Goals:
These goals focus on protecting capital and managing risks. Traders may set goals related to maximum acceptable loss per trade, risk-reward ratios, or keeping drawdowns within a certain percentage.

- Learning and Skill Development Goals:
These goals emphasize continuous learning and skill enhancement.
Traders may set goals to attend seminars, read trading books, acquire new trading techniques, or seek mentorship to improve their trading abilities.

- Portfolio Diversification Goals:
These goals aim to diversify trading activities across different markets, instruments, or strategies.
Traders may set goals to reduce reliance on a single asset or strategy and explore opportunities in diverse markets.

- Time Commitment Goals:
These goals pertain to the time dedicated to trading activities.
Traders may set goals for the number of hours per day or week they will spend on trading, research, or education to maintain a healthy work-life balance.

Example:
Suppose a trader sets the following trading goals:

- Monthly Profitability:
The trader sets a goal to achieve a consistent monthly profit of 5% on their trading capital.

- Risk Management:
The trader establishes a goal to never risk more than 2% of their account balance on any single trade. They also set a risk-reward ratio goal of 1:2, seeking trades where the potential reward is at least twice the amount they are risking.

- Learning and Skill Development:
The trader commits to reading at least one trading book every month and attending a trading seminar or webinar every quarter to enhance their knowledge and skills.

- Diversification:
The trader aims to diversify their portfolio by exploring opportunities in different financial markets such as stocks, forex, and commodities.

- Time Commitment:
The trader sets a goal to spend a minimum of 2-3 hours per day on analyzing the markets, researching potential trades, and reviewing trade outcomes.

These goals provide the trader with a clear roadmap for their trading activities. They serve as a benchmark for assessing progress, making adjustments, and maintaining focus on both profitability and risk management.

It's important to regularly review and evaluate trading goals, ensuring they remain relevant and realistic. As market conditions change or trader experience evolves, goals may need to be adjusted to reflect new aspirations and circumstances.
By setting meaningful and achievable trading goals, traders can ensure a purposeful and focused trading journey, enhancing their chances of success in the markets.

4.2.2 Market Analysis: Determine the methods and tools you will use for market analysis, including technical analysis, fundamental analysis, or a combination of both. Specify the indicators, patterns, or signals you will rely on to identify trading opportunities.

Market analysis is critical for a trading plan as it provides traders with valuable insights into the current and future market conditions. It helps traders make informed decisions, identify potential trading opportunities, and manage risk effectively. Here are some reasons why market analysis is important in a trading plan:

1. Identifying Trading Opportunities: Market analysis allows traders to identify potential trading opportunities based on their preferred trading strategies. By analyzing price movements, chart patterns, technical indicators, or fundamental factors, traders can pinpoint favorable entry and exit points for their trades.

For example, a trader utilizing technical analysis may analyze a chart pattern like a double bottom formation. Market analysis helps the trader identify this pattern and determine the optimal time to enter a trade based on the pattern's confirmation, such as a breakout above the pattern's neckline.

2. Risk Management: Market analysis assists traders in managing risk by providing insights into potential price movements and volatility. By evaluating market conditions, traders can determine appropriate stop-loss levels, position sizes, and risk-reward ratios. For instance, if a trader analyzes market volatility through indicators like Average True Range (ATR), they can adjust their position sizes or stop-loss levels accordingly. If the market is exhibiting higher volatility, the trader may choose to reduce position sizes or widen stop-loss levels to account for the increased risk.

3. Market Context: Market analysis helps traders understand the broader context within which they are operating. By analyzing market trends, support and resistance levels, or fundamental factors, traders gain a comprehensive understanding of the market environment and can make more informed trading decisions.

For example, a trader employing trend-following strategies may analyze the overall market trend using moving averages. By analyzing both short-term and long-term moving averages, traders can determine if the market is in an uptrend or a downtrend, providing a clear direction for their trading decisions.

4. Trade Timing and Execution: Market analysis assists traders in determining the optimal timing for trade entries and exits. By assessing market momentum, volume patterns, or price patterns, traders can make more precise timing decisions to maximize profitability.

For instance, a trader examining price patterns like a bullish flag may analyze market momentum using indicators like the Relative Strength Index (RSI). If the RSI indicates that the market is not yet overbought, the trader may wait for a pullback and employ the flag pattern as a signal for entering a long position.

5. Trade Monitoring and Adjustment: Market analysis allows traders to monitor and adjust their trades as market conditions change. By regularly reviewing and analyzing market developments, traders can make necessary adjustments to their trade management and exit strategies.

For example, a trader may use market analysis to assess whether a trade is still valid and aligns with the prevailing market structure or if adjustments to stop-loss levels or profit targets need to be made based on evolving market conditions.

4.2.3 Entry and exit criteria are essential components of a trading plan as they provide clear guidelines for when to enter and exit trades.

These criteria are based on analysis methods chosen by the trader, which can include specific price thresholds, patterns, or timing indicators.

Here's an example to illustrate how entry and exit criteria work:

1. Entry Criteria:
Entry criteria define the conditions that must be met before entering a trade.
These criteria are determined based on the trader's chosen analysis methods and can be specific price levels, chart patterns, or timing indicators.
Let's consider an example:

Suppose a trader uses technical analysis and identifies a bullish trend in a stock.
Their entry criteria could be defined as follows:

- **Price Threshold:** The trader waits for the stock's price to break above a specific resistance level, such as $50.

Once the price trades above $50 and shows strength in sustaining that level, it triggers a potential entry signal.

- **Bullish Chart Pattern:** The trader looks for bullish chart patterns, such as a bullish engulfing pattern or a breakout from a consolidation phase near the resistance level.

If a valid bullish pattern is observed, it serves as a confirmation for entering the trade.

- **Timing Indicator:** Additionally, the trader may use a timing indicator, such as a stochastic oscillator, to identify oversold conditions within the bullish trend. If the stochastic oscillator shows the stock's price reversing from oversold levels, it can provide an entry signal.

When all the predefined entry criteria are met, the trader considers it an optimal time to enter a long position in the stock.

2. Exit Criteria:

Exit criteria define the conditions under which a trader will exit a trade, either to take profits or to cut losses. Similar to entry criteria, exit criteria can be based on specific price levels, chart patterns, or timing indicators. Let's continue with the previous example:

- Profit Target: The trader sets a profit target based on their analysis, such as a resistance level or a percentage gain. For example, the trader may set a profit target at $55 or a 10% gain from the entry price. Once the stock reaches the predetermined profit target, it triggers an exit signal, and the trader closes the position to secure profits.

- Stop-Loss Placement: To manage risk, the trader sets a stop-loss order at a predetermined price level. This level may be determined by a support level on the chart or a percentage loss the trader is willing to tolerate. If the stock's price reaches the stop-loss level, it triggers an exit signal, and the trader exits the trade to limit losses.

- Reversal Pattern: The trader may also consider exiting a trade if a reversal pattern is observed, signaling a potential trend reversal.

For instance, if the stock exhibits a bearish engulfing pattern or breaks below a key support level, it can indicate weakening bullish momentum, prompting the trader to exit the trade.

By defining clear entry and exit criteria based on their chosen analysis methods, traders can make objective and systematic decisions regarding trade entries and exits.

These criteria help eliminate emotional biases and provide a consistent framework for trade management.

4.2.4 Risk management is a crucial aspect of a trading plan that aims to protect capital and control potential losses.

It involves outlining strategies to manage risk, including determining the maximum acceptable loss per trade, position sizing, stop-loss placement, and evaluating risk-reward ratios.

Here's a simple example to illustrate risk management in trading:

Suppose a trader has a trading account with a total capital of $10,000, and they decide to implement the following risk management strategies:

1. Maximum Acceptable Loss per Trade:
The trader determines that they are willing to risk a maximum of 2% of their trading capital on any single trade.

This means that the maximum acceptable loss per trade is $200 (2% of $10,000).

2. Position Sizing:

The trader uses position sizing calculations to determine the appropriate position size for each trade, based on the maximum acceptable loss per trade.

Let's assume the trader identifies a trade with a potential stop-loss level that would result in a $100 loss if it gets hit.

To adhere to the 2% maximum acceptable loss per trade rule, the trader calculates the position size as follows:

Position Size = Maximum Acceptable Loss per Trade / Potential Loss per Trade
Position Size = $200 / $100 = 2

Therefore, the trader would take a position size equivalent to 2 shares or contracts to limit the potential loss to $100, considering a $100 loss would represent a 2% loss based on their trading capital.

3. Stop-Loss Placement:

The trader determines the appropriate placement of the stop-loss order based on their analysis and risk tolerance.

They set the stop-loss level at a price point that, if reached, would trigger an exit of the trade to limit losses.

In this example, the trader may decide to place the stop-loss order $1 below their entry price.

4. Risk-Reward Ratio:

The trader assesses the risk-reward ratio for each trade, which is the ratio of the potential profit to the potential loss.

For instance, if the trader identifies a profit target of $300 for the trade mentioned above, the risk-reward ratio would be calculated as follows:

Risk-Reward Ratio = Potential Profit / Potential Loss
Risk-Reward Ratio = $300 / $100 = 3:1

A risk-reward ratio of 3:1 means that the potential profit is three times the potential loss. Evaluating potential trades based on favorable risk-reward ratios helps ensure a positive expectancy in the long run.

By implementing risk management strategies like setting a maximum acceptable loss per trade, calculating appropriate position sizes, placing stop-loss orders, and considering risk-reward ratios, traders can protect their capital, limit losses, and maintain a favorable risk profile in their trading activities.

4.2.5 Trade Execution: Define your trade execution plan, including the trading platform, order types, and any specific requirements or protocols you will follow when executing trades.

4.2.6 Trade Recording and Evaluation: Detail how you will record and evaluate your trades. This includes maintaining a trading journal or log to review your decisions, track performance, and make improvements in your trading approach.

4.3: Effective Trade Management Strategies

Successful trade management is crucial for optimizing trade outcomes and profitability. Here are key strategies to consider:

4.3.1 Stop-loss orders are an important risk management tool that traders use to limit potential losses on trades. A stop-loss order is a predetermined price level at which a trader exits a trade if the price moves against their expected direction. Here's an example to illustrate how stop-loss orders work:

Suppose a trader decides to buy shares of a company at $50 per share and sets a stop-loss order at $47 per share. This means that if the stock price drops to or below $47, the stop-loss order will be triggered, and the trader will automatically exit the trade.

In this example, let's consider two scenarios:

Scenario 1: Stop-Loss Order Executed

Shortly after the trader enters the trade, unfavorable news about the company is released, causing the stock price to rapidly decline.

The stock price drops to $46 per share, triggering the stop-loss order at $47.

By having the stop-loss order in place, the trader's potential loss is limited.

Instead of holding onto the trade as the stock price plummets further, the trader exits at $47 per share, limiting the loss to $3 per share.

Scenario 2: Stop-Loss Order Not Executed

In this scenario, the stock performs well after the trader enters the trade. The price increases steadily, reaching $55 per share. Since the stop-loss order is set at $47, which is below the current market price, it remains untriggered.

As the stock continues to rise, the trader may choose to adjust the stop-loss order, either trailing it higher to lock in profits or raising it to limit potential losses. This allows the trader to remain in the trade and capture further gains while protecting against a significant downturn.

Stop-loss orders provide traders with an effective tool for managing risk by preserving capital and limiting losses. By placing a stop-loss order at a predetermined price level, traders can protect themselves against adverse market movements and ensure that their losses are within their acceptable risk thresholds.

It's important to note that while stop-loss orders help manage risk, they are not a guarantee of executing the trade at the exact stop-loss price.

Slippage, which occurs when the market price gaps lower or higher than the stop-loss level, can impact the realized loss.

Traders should consider this possibility and adjust their position sizing and stop-loss placement accordingly.

Overall, incorporating stop-loss orders into a trading plan aids in disciplined trading, risk management, and protecting capital in various market conditions.

4.3.2 Profit targets are predetermined price levels or profit levels that traders set based on their trading plan and analysis.

These targets serve as guidelines for taking profits on trades.

Setting profit targets is essential for maintaining disciplined and objective trading, as it helps traders secure gains and avoid the pitfalls of greed or irrational decision-making.

Let's look at an example to understand how profit targets work:

Suppose a trader identifies a bullish trend in a currency pair and decides to enter a long position at a price of 1.2000. To set a profit target, the trader can consider the following factors:

1. Technical Analysis: The trader analyzes the price chart and identifies a resistance level at 1.2200. This resistance level has acted as a significant barrier in the past, causing the price to reverse or stall.

The trader believes that if the price reaches this level, there is a high probability of a price reversal or a significant pullback.

2. Risk-Reward Ratio: The trader evaluates the risk-reward ratio for the trade.
Let's assume the trader sets a stop-loss order at 1.1950, giving a potential risk of 50 pips.
The trader then decides to set a profit target at 1.2200, providing a potential reward of 200 pips.

With a risk of 50 pips and a reward of 200 pips, the trader has a risk-reward ratio of 1:4.
This means that the potential reward is four times the potential risk for this trade.
In this case, the trader determines that the risk-reward ratio is favorable.

Based on these factors, the trader decides to set the profit target at 1.2200.
This means that once the currency pair reaches the price of 1.2200, the trader will automatically close the trade and secure the profits.

By setting a profit target, the trader ensures that they have a specific level at which they will take profits.

This helps to avoid the temptation of greed and irrational decision-making that may result in giving back gains or missing out on profit opportunities.

It's important to note that while profit targets help traders secure profits, the market may not always reach the target level.

In such cases, traders can reassess the trade and consider adjusting the profit target based on new market developments or technical analysis factors.

Setting profit targets based on a trading plan and analysis provides traders with a disciplined and objective approach to taking profits.

It assists in managing emotions, maintaining consistent trading performance, and aligning trading decisions with desired outcomes.

4.3.3

Trailing stop-loss is a dynamic type of stop-loss order that follows the price as it moves in a favorable direction.

It helps traders protect profits by adjusting the stop-loss level as the trade progresses.

A trailing stop-loss order aims to lock in gains while allowing for potential further upside.

Let's look at an example to understand how trailing stop-loss works:

Suppose a trader buys shares of a company at $50 per share and sets a trailing stop-loss order at $2 below the highest price reached since entering the trade.

The highest price the stock reaches after the trader enters the trade is $60 per share.

As the trade progresses, the stock price starts to rise, reaching $62 per share.

At this point, the trailing stop-loss order adjusts automatically to $60 per share ($2 below the highest price).

If the stock price reverses and drops to $60 per share or below, the stop-loss order is triggered, and the trader exits the trade.

In this scenario, the trailing stop-loss order allows the trader to lock in profits if the price reverses before reaching the initial profit target.

The trader benefits from the upside potential while protecting against a significant downturn or reversal.

Let's consider another example:

Suppose a trader enters a trade with shares of a stock at $100 per share and sets a trailing stop-loss order at a 5% distance from the highest price reached since entering the trade.

If the stock reaches $110 per share, the trailing stop-loss order will automatically adjust to $104.50 per share ($110 - 5% of $110).
If the stock continues to rise and reaches $120 per share, the trailing stop-loss order will adjust to $114 per share ($120 - 5% of $120).

In this example, the trailing stop-loss order allows the trader to capture potential profits in an upward trending market while giving the trade room to breathe. If the stock price reverses and drops below the trailing stop-loss level, the order is triggered, and the trader exits the trade, securing profits.

Trailing stop-loss orders provide traders with a way to protect gains and manage risk while allowing for potential further upside.
They are especially valuable in trending markets, where traders can ride the trend without being stopped out prematurely.

It's important to note that trailing stop-loss orders should be set at an appropriate distance from the highest price reached since entering the trade and should consider the volatility of the market being traded.
Traders must also consider the potential for whipsaws or false moves that might trigger the trailing stop-loss prematurely.

Overall, trailing stop-loss orders offer a dynamic way to protect profits and manage risk in trading, allowing traders to capture potential gains while minimizing the impact of reversals or pullbacks in price.

4.3.4 Position sizing

Position sizing is a critical aspect of risk management that involves determining the appropriate size of each trade based on factors such as risk appetite, probability of success, and market conditions.

It helps traders manage their exposure and ensure that potential losses are within their acceptable risk thresholds.

Here's an example to illustrate how position sizing works:

Suppose a trader has a trading account with a total capital of $10,000 and decides to use a risk management strategy of risking a maximum of 2% of their capital on any single trade.

1. Fixed Dollar Risk:

With a fixed dollar risk approach, the trader determines the maximum amount of capital they are willing to risk on a trade. In this example, the maximum acceptable loss per trade is 2% of $10,000, which equals $200.

To calculate the position size using fixed dollar risk, the trader would divide the maximum acceptable loss per trade by the potential loss per trade. Let's assume the trader identifies a trade with a potential stop-loss level that would result in a $50 loss if hit.

Position Size = Maximum Acceptable Loss per Trade / Potential Loss per Trade

Position Size = $200 / $50 = 4

Based on the fixed dollar risk approach, the trader would take a position size of 4 shares or contracts to ensure that the potential loss is limited to $50 for this trade.

1. Fixed Dollar Risk:

With a fixed dollar risk approach, the trader determines the maximum amount of capital they are willing to risk on a trade.

In this example, the maximum acceptable loss per trade is 2% of $10,000, which equals $200.

To calculate the position size using fixed dollar risk, the trader would divide the maximum acceptable loss per trade by the potential loss per trade.

Let's assume the trader identifies a trade with a potential stop-loss level that would result in a $50 loss if hit.

Position Size = Maximum Acceptable Loss per Trade / Potential Loss per Trade

Position Size = $200 / $50 = 4

Based on the fixed dollar risk approach, the trader would take a position size of 4 shares or contracts to ensure that the potential loss is limited to $50 for this trade.

With a potential loss of $50 per trade, the trader can determine the position size using the fixed dollar risk approach as shown above.

Both the fixed dollar risk and percentage risk per trade approaches ensure that the trader's potential losses are within their predefined risk thresholds. The method chosen depends on the trader's preference and risk management strategy.

By incorporating position sizing techniques into their trading plan, traders can effectively manage their exposure, adhere to their risk management principles, and ensure that potential losses are kept under control. It helps traders strike a balance between risk and reward in their trading activities.

4.3.5 Trade Review and Improvement: Regularly review your trades and performance to identify strengths and weaknesses. Analyze your trade outcomes, assess your decision-making process, and make necessary adjustments to refine and improve your trading strategy.

4.4: Maintaining Discipline and Emotional Control

Maintaining discipline and emotional control is crucial for successful trading. Here are some tips:

4.4.1 Sticking to your trading plan is crucial for consistent and disciplined trading.
It involves adhering to the guidelines and strategies outlined in your plan and avoiding impulsive trading decisions driven by emotions or external factors. Here's why sticking to your plan is important and how it can contribute to trading success:

1. Consistency and Discipline:
Following a well-defined trading plan helps maintain consistency and discipline in your trading activities. It ensures that your decisions are based on a structured approach rather than impulsive reactions to market fluctuations or external influences.

2. Objective Decision-Making:

A trading plan provides a clear framework for making trading decisions based on predetermined criteria and analysis.

By following your plan, you can minimize the impact of emotional biases and make objective decisions aligned with your strategies and goals.

3. Risk Management:

A trading plan incorporates risk management strategies to protect your capital and limit losses. Adhering to these risk management guidelines helps you stay within your predefined risk limits and avoid impulsive, risky trades that could lead to significant losses.

4. Avoiding Emotional Trading: Healthy Mindset and Managing Emotions in Trading

4.4.2 Controlling emotions and maintaining a healthy mindset is critical for successful trading. Emotions can cloud judgment and lead to impulsive decisions, resulting in poor trading outcomes. Developing strategies to manage emotions and foster a healthy mindset is essential for long-term trading success. Here are some key aspects to consider:

1. Self-Awareness:
Understanding your emotions and recognizing how they can impact your trading decisions is the first step towards managing them effectively. Be mindful of emotions such as fear, greed, overconfidence, and impulsiveness. Regular self-reflection and journaling can help you identify patterns and triggers that affect your emotions during trading.

2. Emotional Detachment:
Emotionally detaching yourself from the outcome of each trade can help you make more rational decisions. Instead of focusing solely on individual trades, focus on following your trading plan and executing your strategies consistently. Remind yourself that trading is a probabilistic endeavor, and losses are a natural part of the process.

3. Pre-Trade Preparation: Engage in pre-trade rituals and preparation to cultivate a focused and disciplined mindset. Review your trading plan, analyze the markets, and set realistic expectations. This pre-trade routine helps shift your focus to the process rather than being solely result-oriented.

4. Risk Management: Implementing solid risk management techniques helps mitigate the fear and anxiety associated with potential losses. Set appropriate stop-loss levels and position sizes based on your risk tolerance and trading plan. By having a predetermined risk management strategy in place, you can trade with more confidence and reduce the impact of emotional fluctuations.

5. Educate Yourself: Continuously educate yourself about trading psychology and emotional biases. Understand the common cognitive biases that can influence decision-making, such as confirmation bias or anchoring bias. This knowledge can help you recognize these biases in your thinking and make more objective choices.

6. Positive Self-Talk and Visualization: Practice positive self-talk to reinforce confidence and belief in your abilities as a trader. Visualize successful trades and outcomes to boost your motivation and align your mindset with success. This positive self-talk and visualization can help counteract self-doubt and build resilience in the face of challenges.

7. Take Breaks and Practice Self-Care: Trading can be mentally demanding, so it's important to take regular breaks and engage in self-care activities. Exercise, meditation, and spending time with loved ones can help reduce stress levels and maintain a balanced mental and emotional state. Taking breaks from trading also prevents burnout and allows for perspective.

8. Learn from Mistakes: Embrace mistakes and losses as learning opportunities rather than personal failures. Analyze your trades objectively and focus on identifying areas for improvement. By viewing mistakes as an inherent part of the learning process and adjusting your approach accordingly, you can grow as a trader and build confidence.

Managing emotions and fostering a healthy mindset is an ongoing process that requires self-awareness, practice, and patience. By implementing strategies to control emotions, traders can make more rational and disciplined decisions, enhancing their overall trading performance and long-term success.

Suppose a trader enters a trade with a high level of confidence, having conducted thorough analysis and identified what appears to be a high-probability setup. However, as the trade progresses, the market unexpectedly moves against the trader's position, resulting in a series of consecutive losses.
In this situation, managing emotions becomes crucial. Let's explore how different approaches to handling emotions can influence trading decisions:

1. Emotional Reaction:
The trader reacts emotionally to the losses, experiencing frustration, self-doubt, and fear. Emotions take over, leading to impulsive decision-making. Due to feeling desperate to recover losses quickly, the trader deviates from their trading plan and starts taking trades based on gut feelings or tips from others. This approach further exacerbates losses and may even lead to blowing up the trading account.

2. Healthy Mindset and Emotional Management: The trader, with a healthy mindset, approaches the losses in a more constructive way. They recognize that losses are inevitable in trading and understand that it's a part of the overall journey. By practicing emotional detachment, the trader avoids excessive attachment to individual trades and maintains focus on following their trading plan and executing their strategies consistently.

The trader takes time for self-reflection to identify any emotional triggers that affect their decision-making. Through journaling and analysis, they determine that they may have been overconfident in their initial analysis, and market conditions were not as favorable as they anticipated.

With this awareness, the trader remains disciplined and patient. They review and adjust their trading plan based on the lessons learned from the losses. They reinforce positive self-talk, reminding themselves of their abilities as a trader and taking a long-term perspective.

The trader continues to follow proper risk management techniques, placing reasonable stop-loss levels and position sizes for each trade.
They also engage in self-care activities to manage stress, such as exercise and mindfulness practices.

By maintaining emotional stability and a healthy mindset, the trader avoids making impulsive decisions driven by emotions.
Instead, they learn from their mistakes, adapt their strategies accordingly, and continue trading with renewed focus and resilience.

Ultimately, managing emotions and fostering a healthy mindset allows the trader to navigate challenges, learn from setbacks, and maintain a consistent approach to trading.
It helps to establish a solid foundation for long-term success in the ever-changing world of financial markets.

4.5. Long-Term Perspective:

A trading plan takes into account your long-term goals and strategies.
By following your plan, you maintain focus on the bigger picture and avoid being swayed by short-term market fluctuations or external noise.
This helps you stay on track towards achieving your trading objectives.

4.6. Learning and Improvement:

Sticking to your plan allows you to evaluate the effectiveness of your strategies and make data-driven assessments of your trading performance.
It provides an opportunity to learn from both successful and unsuccessful trades, identify areas for improvement, and refine your trading plan over time.

4.7. Confidence and Trust:

Following your trading plan builds trust in your strategies and enhances confidence in your decision-making. It helps you avoid second-guessing yourself during volatile market conditions or when facing temporary setbacks.
By trusting your plan, you can manage uncertainty and stay focused on your goals.

Remember, a trading plan is a dynamic document that can be adjusted and refined as needed.

However, deviating from your plan should only be done after careful evaluation and consideration, rather than impulsively reacting to market fluctuations or external influences.

Sticking to your trading plan requires self-discipline, patience, and commitment.
It is essential for consistent and successful trading outcomes, helping you navigate the markets in a rational and methodical manner.

By following a disciplined trading plan and implementing effective trade management strategies, traders can increase their chances of consistent profitability and long-term success in the markets.

Regularly review and update your plan as market conditions change, and stay committed to continuous improvement.

Chapter 5: Sustaining Motivation, Setting New Goals, and Embracing Personal Growth

In the journey of trading, sustaining motivation, setting new goals, and embracing personal growth are critical for long-term success and fulfillment.
As a trader, it is important to remain motivated, continuously evolve, and strive for personal growth to navigate the dynamic and ever-changing financial markets.
This chapter delves deeper into strategies and practices to sustain motivation, set new goals, and foster personal growth within the trading journey. Let's explore these aspects in more detail:

1. Reflect on Achievements:

Take time to reflect on your trading achievements and successes. Celebrate your wins, regardless of their size, as they contribute to your overall progress and build confidence. This reflection helps sustain motivation by reminding you of your capabilities, resilience, and progress made over time. Acknowledge the milestones you have achieved and the growth you have attained as a trader.

2. Set New Goals:

Continually setting new goals is essential for maintaining motivation and keeping yourself focused. These goals can be related to improving specific trading skills, increasing profitability, expanding into new markets or asset classes, or developing a diversified trading strategy. Make your goals specific, measurable, achievable, relevant, and time-bound (SMART), and regularly revisit and adjust them as needed. Setting new goals provides a clear sense of direction and purpose, propelling you forward in your trading journey.

3. Learn from Mistakes:

Embrace mistakes as invaluable learning opportunities and use them to grow as a trader. Analyze your losses and understand the reasons behind them. This self-reflection allows you to identify areas for improvement, refine your strategies, and make better decisions in the future. Cultivate a growth mindset that views setbacks as stepping stones to success, and approach them with curiosity and a desire to learn. With each mistake, you gain valuable insights that contribute to your personal growth and development as a trader.

4. Continuous Education:

Commit to lifelong learning and professional development in trading.

Stay updated on market trends, economic news, and new trading techniques through reading books, attending webinars or seminars, and participating in online courses.

Engage in ongoing education to broaden your knowledge base, refine your trading skills, and adapt to changing market dynamics.

Embrace a growth mindset that encourages continuous learning and improvement.

5. Seek Mentorship and Community:

Surround yourself with like-minded individuals who can provide mentorship and support.

Connect with experienced traders, join trading communities or online forums, and participate in workshops or trading groups to share experiences, learn from others, and receive constructive feedback.

Mentors and a supportive community can provide guidance, accountability, and valuable insights that propel your personal growth and trading success.

6. Embrace Technology and Innovation:

Stay abreast of technological advancements and innovative tools that can enhance your trading capabilities.

Explore new trading platforms, software, or algorithms that align with your trading strategies and objectives.

Embracing technology and innovation can improve your efficiency, expand your trading options, and increase your ability to adapt to market changes. By adopting cutting-edge tools, you position yourself for continued growth and success.

7. Practice Self-Care:

Prioritize your well-being and practice self-care to maintain a healthy mindset.

Trading can be mentally and emotionally demanding, so it is essential to take breaks and engage in activities that recharge and rejuvenate you.

Incorporate exercise, meditation, mindfulness, hobbies, or spending quality time with loved ones into your routine.

By taking care of your physical, mental, and emotional well-being, you optimize your performance, decision-making, and overall trading experience.

8. Journaling and Track Your Progress:

Maintain a trading journal to record your trades, emotions, and lessons learned.

Regularly review your journal to track your progress, identify patterns, and refine your trading approach.

Journaling provides a valuable record of your experiences, helping you identify your strengths, weaknesses, and areas for improvement.

Through this self-reflection, you enhance self-awareness, make data-driven decisions, and encourage personal growth as a trader.

9. Adapt and Evolve:

Recognize that the markets are dynamic, and strategies that worked in the past may become less effective over time.

Stay flexible and open to adapting your trading approach to accommodate evolving market conditions and trends.

Embrace new technologies, research, or trading styles that align with your goals and are in line with prevailing market dynamics.

Continual adaptation, learning, and evolution are key components of sustained success in trading.

10. Cultivate Resilience and Embrace Challenges:

Develop resilience and embrace challenges as opportunities for growth.

Trading can present both successes and setbacks, but it is how you respond to these challenges that matters.

Build mental and emotional resilience by reframing setbacks as learning experiences, maintaining a positive attitude, and focusing on solutions rather than dwelling on the problem.

Embracing challenges with the mindset of personal growth enables you to overcome obstacles and emerge stronger as a trader.

Sustaining motivation, setting new goals, and embracing personal growth are integral components of achieving long-term success and fulfillment in trading.

By nurturing your motivation, continuously setting new goals, and fostering personal growth, you create a solid foundation for ongoing development and improvement.

Embrace the journey, invest in your growth, and embrace personal transformation as you navigate the dynamic world of trading.

These examples demonstrate how traders can sustain motivation, set new goals, and embrace personal growth within their trading journeys. By incorporating these practices, traders can stay motivated, adapt to evolving market conditions, and continue progressing toward their goals while experiencing personal growth along the way.

1. Example of Sustaining Motivation:
After experiencing a series of losses, a trader feels demoralized and discouraged. To sustain motivation, they reflect on their previous successes and remind themselves of the progress they have made. They review their trading journal, celebrate past profitable trades, and recognize their ability to overcome challenges. By focusing on their achievements and reminding themselves of their capabilities, they reignite their motivation to continue trading and improve their performance.

2. Example of Setting New Goals:

A seasoned trader has consistently achieved their financial goals and is looking to set new targets. They decide to expand their trading strategies by learning and incorporating options trading into their portfolio. They research options strategies, take educational courses, and practice simulated trading to develop proficiency in this new area. By setting a goal to master options trading, they stay motivated, broaden their skill set, and create opportunities for additional profits.

3. Example of Embracing Personal Growth:

A trader realizes that their risk management skills need improvement after a series of significant losses. They commit to embracing personal growth and invest time in learning and practicing proper risk management techniques. They seek mentorship from experienced risk managers, read books on risk control, and use trading simulators to refine their risk assessment abilities. By proactively addressing their weakness, they develop resilience, improve their ability to protect capital, and experience personal growth as a trader.

4. Example of Continuous Education:

An intermediate trader wants to stay updated on the latest market trends and strategies.

They regularly attend trading webinars, enroll in online courses, and join trading forums to engage with other traders.

By staying knowledgeable about market dynamics and incorporating new information into their trading strategies, they maintain a competitive edge and continually improve their trading skills.

5. Example of Adaptive Approach:

A trader recognizes that their current trading strategy is no longer as effective due to changing market conditions.

They adapt their approach by exploring other asset classes and looking for alternative trading opportunities.

By expanding into different markets or adjusting their strategies to suit the prevailing conditions, they remain adaptable, avoid becoming stagnant, and find new avenues for success.

Remember, your journey as a trader is unique. By sustaining motivation, setting meaningful goals, and embracing continuous learning, you can cultivate long-term success and fulfillment in your trading career. Draw inspiration from these examples and chart your own path to a prosperous and fulfilling trading journey.

Wishing you all the best and may your trading path be one of personal growth, lifelong learning, and abundant success.

In closing, I want to extend my sincerest gratitude to all the traders who have embarked on this journey with me. Your dedication, perseverance, and passion for the markets are truly inspiring. Remember that success in trading is not just about profits and losses; it's about personal growth, discipline, and continuous learning. Embrace the challenges, stay focused on your goals, and never stop believing in your ability to achieve greatness. Thank you for joining me on this incredible adventure, and may your trading endeavors be filled with prosperity, joy, and fulfillment. Happy trading!

Luna Marlowe